INTIMATE

CONVERSATIONS

WITH THE AWAKENER

INTIMATE
CONVERSATIONS
WITH THE AWAKENER

BAL NATU

1998

Sheriar Foundation

ISBN: 1-880619-22-9

Other books by Bal Natu:
Conversations with The Awakener (1991)
More Conversations with The Awakener (1993)

Dedicated to You,
The Awakener
of
All Hearts

and to
all those who are seeking Union
with You,
the "Eternally Benevolent"

It is not with my eyes
that I see You.
It is not with my ears
that I hear You.
Only with the eyes and ears of the heart
do I listen and view,
Love's pure gift granted by You.
Silence is the breath of Your being.
To fathom its glory I sing.
May these offerings Your heart delight,
and Your glance drown me in Your Ocean of light.

Contents

Preamble

Oh Awakener, Who are You? To me, You are the ever fresh presence of Love, pure and boundless, that sustains and quickens life on all its levels. Although formless, You are vibrant in all forms, transcendent yet incarnate. Your grace is unconditional. So, irrespective of any merits, with the slightest sincere yearning, You are equally available for help to one and all. In a way, You are even impatient to awaken our hearts more and more to Your pure Love on our journey to You. You are the one and only Awakener.

Being Infinite, in Your Oceanic originality, You have planted the seed of original nature in each one's heart, and You nurture these seeds through the course of countless life events, so that they may germinate, blossom, and fructify in their own season.

Since the moment, pregnant with Your grace, that You first drew me into the orbit of Your Love, naturally I have not felt the urge to follow anyone, nor do I expect anyone to follow me. This graceful dispensation has helped me to refrain from judging or imitating others. Once one is set upon one's natural path, the various, wondrous talents of others can unfold to one's deep appreciation without being enticed by them. As a result, a reciprocal relationship of pure love and resignation to Your wish naturally begins to blossom.

Everyone's life is Your gift, sustained by Your grace, love, and compassion. Hence, I do not wish to be a mentor or guide — just a friend to fellow wayfarers on their journey to You. And in this spirit of simple friendship I offer these conversations, not with insistence to convince anyone, but as a pleasant way of sharing my perceptions on life to the extent I have absorbed them in Your company. Such playful dialogues with You are a form of heart-to-heart communication, a life of ever fresh delight.

I have chosen to describe our conversations as "intimate" to indicate an intimacy without the least hesitation, whether we are speaking of matters trifling or profound. In some conversations ideas flow naturally, one from another, while in others they may seem disconnected. Some of our talks are brief yet intense; some are long and serious; some are humorous also. Through these conversations, You have delightfully revealed some insights about Your relationship to me. You were not at all annoyed by my sometimes childish, silly questions; instead, with an uncanny knack, You responded patiently, and often with lively humor.

If these musings within my heart happen to help anyone in finding or arriving at a more intimate relationship with You, that too is a part of Your Game and grace. All threads are in Your hand. For the life of me, I shall never be able to fathom or really share the depth of Your loving concern for me. In fact, the immensity of each of Your noble attributes is so great, that sometimes I have to laugh at my poor attempts to capture any of them in words.

As it is far beyond my mind to grasp the immeasurable magnitude of Your Game, I frankly admit my inability to express adequately through these conversations the feelings that Your tender, timeless words have awakened within my heart. I must honestly acknowledge that many a time I have failed to present the depth of Your statements, and express accurately the import that You wished to convey. So, in sharing these vignettes, I might have missed the mark. After all, they are just my immature attempts to convey what I have gathered or understood. For such inaccuracies, I beg Your pardon, and also request the reader to bear with my incompetence. However, if these fragmentary attempts manage to convey even a whiff of Your loving presence, I shall feel immensely grateful to You, the Source of Love, unfettered and unbounded.

Had not a few of my close friends helped me in typing and editing these conversations with You, as they were sporadically unfolding in my heart, the first scribbled pages would never have seen the light of day. My warmest and most sincere thanks to them, my co-workers. And I, along with my friends, wholeheartedly invite and welcome the reader to join me, with an open mind, in sharing this intimacy with The Awakener, which is the essence of these conversations. Thanks.

Hooray!

February 25, 1998   *Bal Natu*

Return to the Center

We were sitting quietly side by side under a grand old oak. It had a thick, round trunk, and its drooping branches with their waxy green leaves formed a sheltering umbrella over us. The charm and majesty of the old tree emanated across the grassy slope. The meadow below seemed to rest pleasantly under the sky, and patches of grass were sparkling in the soft sunlight just peering over the horizon. The breeze was cool and bracing.

You tapped me gently on my shoulder and remarked, "Today you seem to be blissfully quiet. I am happy."

As I heard You say this, I wondered whether You were purposely veiling Your omniscience or trying to get a rise out of me. At that moment, in spite of being surrounded by such majestic scenery and with You sitting beside me, I was feeling too drained and exhausted to converse on any subject. What an irony!

Without looking at You, I blurted out, "On the contrary, I feel fed up with my life and even with this human body!"

You laughed heartily without reprimand and said, "You are not fed up with the body at all. Rather, you are feeling frustrated owing to the unfulfillment of your deep-rooted desires. Were they gratified, you would love even to be a centenarian!"

You had diagnosed my disease without condemning it. "You are not totally wrong," I admitted, "but why should I have this body at all? That is the question that so often bothers me."

Your tranquil eyes sparkled as You lovingly replied, "The purpose of having a human body is to understand, feel, and realize the blissful, formless, Infinite Spirit ever residing within you, that I am. In fact, the Spirit is eager, even impatient, but it does not impose Itself. It is waiting for your wholehearted consent so that It can begin to reveal Itself more and more."

Incredible words! I drew a deep, excited breath. "I am ready for such an unfolding right now!"

You flashed a smile and said, "In the first place, understanding the paramount importance and function of the human body must become a longing of the heart, an intense passion."

I was silenced momentarily, then confessed, "I am neither one-pointed nor resolute in the intention I have just expressed. However, the conflict within me seems to originate in Your infinite, formless spirit manifesting in an endless variety of fascinating forms."

An affectionate glow lit Your face. "Perhaps you do not correctly understand what you are saying. The main reason is that your mind is 'hydra-headed,' so you are unable to make any firm decision that is close to your original nature. And this impedes the blossoming of life."

"What do You mean by this?"

You gracefully raised Your face, peering into my eyes as You spoke. "Blossoming is a very natural and delicate process of gradually becoming aware of My presence within you. It's a game I play through everyone. And each one has a free choice as to whether to play along. It is difficult for Me to describe this process in words. It is an art of abiding joyfully, without inner resistance to the numberless laws of nature that are operating in and through your life."

Your explanation deeply touched my heart and I pleaded, "Please guide me to play well and fair with You. And in case I am blessed with a little success in improving my game, what shall the result be?"

"A surprise!" And with a benign dignity You added, "Anyone who is sincerely open to My guidance shall soon witness that attending to the daily chores of one's life will not be a drudgery, but a life filled with simple uplifting moments of selfless joy."

"Really!" I exclaimed. "Whenever I hear such words of

cheer from You, I'm inspired to begin instantly!"

You glanced lovingly at me, and in a warm voice You went on, "Then why don't you begin and find the result for yourself?"

My old nature of self-defense was revived, and I said, "Do you mean to say that I have not tried?"

"You have, but not the way you should."

"Sorry. After all, I am an ordinary human being, and as they say: 'To err is human.'" I was still trying to justify my folly.

You gave me a deep, steady look. "Now listen. First you have to forget — I mean try to forget the past — and I will help you."

"How?" I asked excitedly.

"Not by brooding over what you have done or what you should not have done. If such thoughts assail you, offer them to Me. With unadulterated trust in Me, this practice will gradually make you feel lighthearted. This will encourage you to offer more of your thoughts to Me. And I especially love for you to share even your most commonplace thoughts and concerns."

"When can I start?" I asked urgently. But the next moment I regretted my impatience. I was still caught up in my habitual impetuousness.

Rich in sympathy, you calmly replied, "There is no more auspicious moment than now — the ever-renewing Now. In this timeless moment, all moments of all times are included, not differentiated. Begin!" You gazed benignly at me.

"You know well that I am an average person." I implored, "Can You tell me something that I can both under-stand and follow?"

Your glowing eyes shone like stars, and You answered: "Just start to witness whatever is happening within you and around you, which is only the periphery of life, and return to the Center, which I am. This is the way to grow in My pres-ence. Let this be your deep passion, your sole focus. Now I have opened the door for you. Whether to walk in or stay out — I leave that to you."

With these enlightening and inviting words, You stood up and with regal, graceful strides, walked away from the tree.

As I witnessed You going, I felt that something divinely monumental had occurred, and I was wondering whether You were walking outside or inside of me.

Your words, "Return to the Center," seemed to surcharge the entire atmosphere around me. I felt those same words echoing and re-echoing from within the trunk of the dear old oak tree I was leaning against. And as I looked out upon the meadow, every leaf of grass seemed to be singing in unison the same refrain:

"Just witness and return to the Center . . .
the Center!"

Passage to the Presence

By any normal standard it was a splendid morning. The air was filled with the sweet notes of birds, and the gentle glow of dawn poured through the window onto the table as I finished my breakfast. But I was in no mood to enjoy the beauty of that atmosphere. On the table before me was a disorderly clutter of notes and memoranda — my tasks for the day.

"Lord, what a muddle!" I thought miserably. "How oppressive these petty worldly affairs can be!"

There was enough tea left in the pot for one more cup before I began my dreary labors. But as I started to pour, the lid slipped from the pot, crashed against the edge of the table, and fell to the floor. Grumbling, I pushed back my chair and got down on my hands and knees to retrieve it.

When I got back to my feet, I saw You there, standing across from me, calmly tidying up the mess on the table. When least expected, but perhaps most needed, You cheer me with Your visits. I watched in wonder as Your graceful hands straightened a stack of papers, refastened the lid to the sugar jar — which I had screwed on crookedly — and folded the napkin I had left crumpled by my cup. With Your arrival, some fresh vitality seemed to burst forth in the room.

You glanced up with a benign smile and asked me, "How is life?"

"Well, You see how it is with me," I replied in exasperation.

With a playful but meaningful look You said, "If in your life you allow the insignificant to become significant, you will find that even ordinary chores and duties become channels to feel My loving presence."

"In an abstract sense, this may be true. But I must confess that . . ." Just then, with embarrassment, I realized that I hadn't offered You a chair. "Please sit down and be comfortable," I implored.

You adjusted the teapot on the tray, then pulled back a chair and sat down with an air of tranquillity and ease.

"Yes, what You say is right," I stammered. "But the problem is, how can I make it all real for myself?"

With welcoming eyes and a radiant smile, You answered, "Start to remember Me at the beginning and also at the end of every major activity of your daily routine. Then you will notice that I am also participating with you. Can you do this? Occasionally, My intimate response will flood your being. The wonder and joy of such moments will make the most tiresome tasks interesting."

1 CONVERSATIONS with The Awakener

"This sounds quite promising," I said, feeling relaxed and relieved.

My reaction seemed to prompt You to delve deeper into the subject. "Subtler than space, finer than time, My presence is ever-accessible, though not necessarily easy to reach. Silent dialogue with Me is one of the ways of feeling My presence. If your inner attention is focused on Me, you will sense a delicate tug within you, regardless of the activity you are engaged in. And you will become aware that I am caring for you, anxious to help you. No activity is insignificant."

"I am thankful to You for revealing this to me," I replied. And I gazed at You, longing to know more. "My problem is my inability to apply this in my daily life."

"To be practical, start with any ordinary activity, like slipping into your clothes, lifting a spoon, or putting a pen to paper. The world divides activities into 'big' and 'small,' 'important' and 'unimportant,' 'serious' and 'trivial,' and prefers one to the other. But life is one undivided whole. I am very pleased when you remember Me during very ordinary actions." Smiling, You asked, "And do you know why?"

"Why?"

"Because your 'I-ness' is most deeply and firmly rooted in ordinary things."

"Yes, in most small things I feel I am capable of managing on my own."

"But you should feel deep in your heart that you need Me

in them as well. Call on Me in the little — nay, in the littlest — things that you do. For then they sprout tiny yet mighty wings which will gracefully transport you to the higher and subtler realms of My presence within you."

You paused, then with a gentle smile resumed, "The moment you turn to Me, you receive My immediate attention. This may sound easy, but, due to age-old habit, the mind is burdened by numberless nonsensical thoughts and distractions, which constrict your awareness and misdirect your energy. So to become aware of My presence, you must be mindful of your intentions and faithful in your longing to feel Me. And if you do this, you will find that the fulfillment you once derived from a variety of scattered interests is now marvelously contained in Me. But to experience this, you have to listen attentively to the promptings of your own heart, for that is where I am eagerly waiting to speak to you. Then there will blossom within you that quality of openheartedness which tries to hide nothing from Me."

Your love-filled words drenched every part of my being, and I was transported for a while to another realm. "If only I could feel with certainty that You definitely know what I need better than I do myself. When will I feel this?" My heart felt a gentle anguish of longing.

"I know when" — Your eyes sparkled with merriment — "but I won't tell you in advance."

"May it become ingrained in me that whatever pleases You is best for me. In any case, Your reminder to call on You for help in all things, big and small, has eased my mind and lit for me a beacon to lead me through the muddle of mundaneness. I need You — Your fatherly guidance and motherly love — to make more and more room in my heart for You alone. I am sure Your help in my life, with all of its 'pieces,' will reveal a marvelous design of Your love for me."

You looked pleased, and with a simple nod of Your head, You acknowledged my heartfelt adoration. When You stood up to leave, You looked majestic, though at the same time I noticed a mischievous sparkle in Your eyes. Pointing at the things on the table, You winked at me and said, "Wash the dishes, clean and dry them softly as if you were offering your prayers to Me. Attend to your bills and memoranda as though you were doing all that business for Me. Don't divide life into the temporal and the spiritual. I am the Indivisible One."

With a radiant, reassuring glance, You gently passed out of sight. But Your marvelous presence lingered and filled the room with an indescribable bliss. And in Your remembrance, as I set out to attend to my ordinary chores, they began to reveal a fresh aspect of Your presence.

I felt deep within me that You had not only directed me to the passage leading to Your presence, but had even provided me with the visa for my journey. In truth, You are the passage, and You are the Abode. Let the flow of my life be the flow of Your grace. Come and drown me in the Ocean of Your graceful presence.

"Go Slow . . . Stay Low"

"Go slow . . . go slow . . . go slow . . ." Three times I heard these words spoken softly in a captivating, melodious voice. Fascinated, I looked around the room to discover the source of the voice, but to no avail. It seemed to be rhythmically reverberating from every surface.

And then suddenly, looking fresh and vibrant, You entered the room with Your steady, regal gait, Your hands swinging gracefully at Your sides. Beside myself with happiness and surprise, I greeted You effusively. I respectfully motioned for You to sit.

With a mischievous glint in Your eye, You said, "You seem to be in a state of astonishment over something." And feigning ignorance, as usual, You added, "Any particular reason?"

"Just now I heard a voice," I gasped. "It sounded like it was coming from every part of the room."

"I see," You chuckled. "A voice! And what did it say?"

"It said, 'Go slow... go slow... go slow...' like the refrain of a delightful folk song I had never heard before. Do these words carry some special message for me?"

Your eyes flashed. "Surely they do!"

"Then what is it? And where did the voice come from?"

"The voice was the singing of your innermost Being," You answered.

I stared at You, expressing my incomprehension. You continued, "There are innumerable levels of life within you, within everyone. The life of every individual possesses a deep, latent longing to know its own origin. It was this life within you that you heard calling to you."

"I don't really understand what you mean by 'inner layers,'" I said, feeling somewhat self-conscious for being so obtuse.

You gave me a reassuring look and replied, "These layers, and there are many of them, are composed of your deep-rooted thoughts and feelings — lust, jealousy, anger, pride, boredom, complacency, romance, revenge, serious inquiry, idle inquisitiveness, and so forth. Most of the time one or more of these layers prevent one from experiencing the joy of unfettered inner life."

"So what is to be done about this?" I asked. "To some extent I can understand what You are saying, as I am becoming aware of a few conflicts within myself which seem to inhibit my own capacity to experience the joy in life. How can I discover this unfettered joy You mention?"

In a convincing yet gentle tone, You said, "There are many outward paths one can follow, but they all point to the same secret. The secret is the individual's total commitment and wholehearted dedication to whatever goal he or she seeks, as long as that goal does not include any thought of self-interest.

"No one's life may be treated as totally unspiritual. It is the spirit of selfless dedication which makes any way of life spiritual and leads to a natural unfolding of the subtle, inner realities. With the passage of time, enriched by sincerity and honesty, one is prompted to explore the inner realms of life from which this spirit of dedication springs forth.

"Thus in a graceful and natural way, one comes closer to traversing the 'Royal Path' of invoking Me and imploring My help in one's honest inquiry into the essence of life.

"Calling on Me helps to shed unwanted burdens gathered during the initial pursuit of external goals. One begins to feel light in heart and mind. Gradually, the burden of thoughts and feelings falls away, the clouds of confusion disperse. This marks the auspicious moment when one's perspective shifts from outer to inner. One becomes ready to accept life anew, with openness of mind."

You smiled playfully and added, "First I come into your heart, and then slowly enter your life. This happens without your being aware of it. Don't forget, I remember you before you remember Me."

I confessed meekly, "I know this, and even feel ashamed of it. But why not remind me to remember You *before* You remember me?"

"Hmm . . . That's a good question," You admitted, looking serious for a moment. But then You suddenly smiled and added, "However, I leave you to find out the answer." We both laughed.

Before our laughter faded, I began, "This seems to be one of Your ancient habits — to reveal a tiny bit and conceal the greater part of the secret."

"But don't you think it's also one of My most effective ways of awakening your trust in My love for you?"

I smiled in appreciation of Your humor. "Now I understand where the words 'go slow' came from — the source of life within me seeking its origin. But what do they mean?"

"They mean to go slow with your thoughts and feelings. It is only when you slow down that the secrets of life can begin to reveal themselves to you. But you have to understand that going slow isn't the same as 'moving slowly.' To go slow means to stay centered in My remembrance. It means honoring every activity by giving each its full measure of attention. Perhaps you may wonder how this is done." You paused for a moment and added, "By bringing body, mind, and heart into harmony. Once this harmony is established, then even the most rapid movements of a dancer or an athlete are 'slow' because they are totally centered in the moment."

"But what is harmony?"

A look of bemused contemplation came over Your face, then faded as You continued, "When there is no conflict between thoughts, feelings, and activities, they express themselves in one resonance. That is harmony. Moments of harmony are precious offerings to Me. For example, if you wish to give something to someone you love, you take great care in order to please that person. So it's natural that if you wish to live for Me, your first concern should be to please Me."

I have often noticed that giving detailed metaphysical explanations seems to bore You, whereas You delight in conversing on everyday subjects. You began to look withdrawn, as if You had lost interest in the subject, and You gazed through the window for some moments, studying something which was not apparent to me. You brushed Your fingers through Your hair and then paced up and down the room a couple of times. Then You returned to Your seat, and continued:

"With this harmony, you will find that life takes on a subtler, more precise rhythm. You become aware of the sheer immensity of life, with its diversity and interconnectedness; this very awareness, in itself, will help you to avoid fixed ideas and dogmas.

"My ever-renewing presence turns life into a lively, ever-changing game. But this can only happen when your acceptance of My presence does not require any kind of external prop. This acceptance gives you the confidence to face life —

no matter what happens to you or around you. You should know that My presence is like the very sky above you, ever spanning beyond the horizon of your awareness."

A feeling of awe came over me; Your words had such power that I was totally silent within and without. It was a unique experience.

As You smiled, Your mood again changed, and very casually You said, "A time will come when you will go so slow that you won't be concerned about what will happen even in the next moment."

The improbability of this made me think You were joking somehow, and I chuckled, "But how could someone live like that? Wouldn't life come to a standstill and stagnate?"

"Oh no," You replied, looking serious again, "at that point, I naturally take over what you have trustingly relinquished to Me."

Something clicked within me, and I understood a little of what You were conveying. I exclaimed, "And from then on we will journey together! Wonderful!"

"But it's not as easy as you may think," You cautioned. You paused for what seemed to be a timeless moment and, giving me a probing look, added, "Stay low."

These two words began to vibrate within me, gathering the same force as the two words I'd heard earlier. Just then, You rose to leave.

"Wait!" I pleaded. "Won't You tell me what You mean by these words?"

The corners of Your eyes crinkled merrily, and You said, "No, not now. However, I will give you a hint: to find Me, the Most High, it is absolutely necessary for you to stay low. You have to try to stay low more and more."

"But what do You mean by staying low?"

"To stay low is to perceive My glory in everyone and everything and to honor it with all respect. It is to be conscious that My glory is the source and foundation of perception itself. As for the rest, you will have to discover that on your own."

And You gave me an affectionate look.

At that moment my mind seemed to go blank. And yet, as though from nowhere, words came to me.

"You mean I should be like the most insignificant particle of dust, totally helpless under the immensity of the open sky? I should be resigned completely to Your divine game?"

Your beautiful eyes gleamed with delight, and as You left, Your glowing glance filled my being with ineffable joy.

Whenever I try to recapture the memories of Your visits, I am flooded with the sublime feelings that sweep over me as we converse. By Your Grace, may I become a little more aware, with each visit, that You and You alone are the conductor of the symphony of my life. Written words cannot be more than a poor substitute for that melody and music. "Please guide me to play in tune with Your music. Will this bring a smile to Your face?"

The Interminable Journey

I thought it would be fun to journey with You, and so it was, at the beginning. But after a time I began to complain and grumble, and I would hear You saying, "Have a little more patience, a little more trust in Me." But this did not seem to pick me up. To cultivate that little bit of patience and trust that You expected of me was a difficult job. My spirits sagged and my heart became heavy.

I remembered when I had been happy, so happy, to walk with You hand in hand. I had thought that would continue until eternity. I don't know why and how things began to change, but those changes began to unsettle my relationship with You. It was hard to cope with the new situations that confronted me, and I began to feel tired and exhausted, weak and helpless. However, sometimes I would visualize that, with my hand barely clutching Your shoulder, I was being dragged along after You.

When I had walked beside You in earlier times, my eyes had been greeted by panoramic vistas of forests and pastures, dales and hills. Now, as my eyes have grown weak and have lost their distant vision, I walk with my head lowered, able to see only a few feet in front of me. But on a few occasions, what beautiful heavens are reflected in the dust of the path! These scenes are even more beautiful than those that I had previously witnessed. I ask myself whether these visions are real or just daydreams — I cannot tell.

So unfathomable are Your ways, it is hard to say anything about You. You are so close, so close and yet it seems impossible for me even to touch You. How, then, am I to catch hold of You?

But I am always grateful for Your timely flashes that lead me out of my confusion. Now I realize my impudence in presuming that I, on my own, could hold Your hand. For it is always You who hold me, and it is Your unconditional compassion that sustains me in my seemingly interminable journey to You.

Let my trust in You sink its roots into the whole soil of my being.

Your Smiling Presence

It was midnight but I could not get a wink of sleep. A month earlier I had had a very nasty motorcycle accident. My right leg was now in a splint and I had a deep wound in my thigh. The pain was intense and sometimes unbearable. I sat on the edge of my bed and balanced my right leg on a stool, while my left dangled over the edge.

It was a cool November night and the leaves on the trees outside my window were softly rustling as if to soothe me with their sound. The new moon shone down on me through the fleecy clouds with a gentle light, as if it were silently expressing its sympathy for my plight. On the table in my room, the night lamp cast a pleasantly dim light through its colored silken shade. A glass of water had been set out and my comfortably cushioned crutches were near at hand. Everything around me was imbued with a quiet beauty and conspired to give me comfort, but I could not appreciate any of it.

My visits to the hospital had exhausted me and left me anxious and depressed. Alone in my room, I was easily carried away by my worst imaginings. Instead of inhaling the perfume of a flower bouquet of trust in You, I allowed myself to wallow in the backwaters of depression. I wondered whether my wound would heal or if it would become infected. If it became infected, would my leg have to be amputated? Would I then be able to continue my present job? If I lost my job, how could I ever hope to pay for the staggering medical bills I had accumulated in such a short time?

Part of me realized that most of this worrying was nonsensical, but I found myself waist-deep in this quagmire of self-pity and concern, and could not extricate myself. It was then that You entered the room and beamed a radiant smile. Taking a seat, You said, "As you cannot walk freely, I decided to walk right in." The room was brightened by Your exhilarating, charming smile. It was so intense that I was instantly lifted out of my low spirits. I felt as if I were completely healed and could even run a mile.

Glancing at me, you asked, "What happened to your leg? You're looking weak and worried."

Your questions brought me down from my feeling of exaltation, and I narrated the whole episode of the accident. Looking compassionately at me, You said, "Now that this has happened, don't brood over it. Continue to do what is necessary. Do you need any help from Me?"

Since I had been worrying almost constantly about my health and financial situation, it was with only a little hesitancy that I replied, "Now that You have asked, may I request good health?"

"Why not?" You answered.

"And more wealth?" I added with a little uncertainty.

"Sure, sure," You responded magnanimously.

"I have already implored You many times for these gifts," I protested, stammering slightly at my own boldness.

"Yes, you have," You calmly replied.

"But I have not yet been given . . . !"

"Right," You said in an unruffled manner.

"But why didn't You help me when I asked for it previously?" I complained.

With a serious look You said, "Because I love you so much."

Surprised, I exclaimed, "I was suffering and You did not pay heed! What sort of love is this?"

"It is Selfless Love," You said, in the same calm, matter-of-fact tone. "I suffer in you to reveal the source of unfading and unending bliss — the real health and treasure that is within you."

For some moments a wonderful silence prevailed. I did not — rather, could not — respond, for I was trying to absorb the import of Your words. Your intimate, benign smile silenced my mind.

Knowing that I was now more receptive, You continued, "Don't get disheartened in your life. Don't become overenthusiastic either. Try to remain poised in My remembrance and maintain a balance in your thoughts and feelings. Watch the unfolding of your life dispassionately, and you will discover My help even in the midst of the most mundane happenings."

I was fascinated by what You were revealing to me. You seemed pleased by my interest and continued:

"Listen. There are innumerable seasons in everyone's life. Things pass and then return, though slightly changed. This cycle of blossoming and withering is indispensable. Life's journey through these opposites is enriched and, if accepted in the right understanding, leaps ahead toward new horizons.

"Suffering and pain are as inevitable as moments of joy and delight. This is the very fabric of life. Pass through it all, and eventually joy and suffering will merge into one harmonious whole, redolent with My love. You will gain this perspective more quickly if you resign to My will, which continually works to reveal to you the everlasting fountain of bliss which I am."

The immensity of Your statements was hard for me to take in, and just then there was a shooting pain in my leg. Discouraged again, I said, "So, You're trying to tell me that all my suffering is necessary?"

You knew what made me blurt out this impertinent question, and ignoring my irritation, You answered, "Not only was this accident necessary for you, but nothing that happens to you is unnecessary. If you only try, with detachment, to understand the meaning behind these events, then life itself will begin to answer your questions."

Then, referring to my earlier request, You added, "Have you searched your mind and heart as to the real reason you were asking for health and wealth? Behind your desire to get better and pay your bills, wasn't there a craving to indulge more and more in worldly pleasures?"

I could not deny this. I realized, as You said it just how attached I was to the world and how strong a pull its attractions and promises had on me, so I kept quiet.

"As for your physical pain," You went on in a humorous vein, "if I drive it out of you, perhaps you may drive Me away as well." You glanced at my cast. "After all, when things go wrong you remember Me, but when things go smoothly you forget Me. Am I right?"

I didn't answer.

"If I were to grant your wishes, you would be attacked from all sides by innumerable temptations. If you succumbed to them, they would only tighten the bonds of ignorance about your true nature. Do you really want that?"

The answer was plain, and You continued in a reassuring and lighthearted way, "I don't mean you have to be grim and serious all the time. In My remembrance, innocent, selfless delight keeps the heart awake to higher values and will enable you to enjoy the game of life."

Then You winked at me. "Do you ever ask Me to help free you from lust and greed with even one percent of the intensity with which you call on Me for physical relief and riches? Do you ever ask Me to get rid of your arrogance and pride with the same wholehearted craving with which you sometimes ask for ice cream or dessert?"

I was crestfallen. What could I say? You had put Your finger on the right spot. But then, to cheer me up, You added, "What I said is not meant to blame you. I understand your limitations and abilities better than you do. What you have done is okay with Me, but you should honestly accept the facts as they are, and in the future try earnestly to transcend your lower desires and be more watchful over your wants and cravings. This will open the door to your inner journey to Me."

Your words were like soothing music that moves the heart even when the mind does not understand what is happening. I felt as if parts of my life which had been restricted, tangled up in crooked knots, were now beginning to be untied. I vainly sought for words to express my indebtedness to You.

But before I could say anything, You got up and very lovingly said, "Every moment in time holds chalices of holy wine, and every point in space contains unknown delightful heavens. But I am not going to deal with that topic today. You have had enough of My words for now, don't you think? Good night, and have a restful sleep."

So saying, You walked over to the table and had a sip of water from the glass. Then, pointing to the crescent moon that was clearly visible through the window, You said, "Isn't that lovely?"

I turned my head to look, and at the same moment I saw You shooting out through space to reappear, sitting in the center of the crescent, casually dangling Your left leg. Were You playfully teasing me because I had been sitting in this position when You came in the room? Your wit and wisdom, your humor and compassion — each outdoes the other.

I turned my head to find out whether You were really on the moon or still near the table. I didn't see You anywhere, but the whole room was suffused with Your luminous, loving smile. In an astonished yet exalted mood, I limped over to the table and drank the water You had sipped. It was now "holy wine," and "delightful heavens" seemed to dance around me.

Your every visit is a unique occurrence, with glorious facets. Filled with wonder and delight, I lay on my bed, beside myself with rapture. Turning my head to the crescent moon, I implored You, "Pray, graciously pour Your smiling presence into my entire being. That would be a sure remedy for any malady — physical or mental. The perfect panacea — Your smiling presence!"

Acceptance, Not Annoyance

I was sitting on a bench in a quiet corner of the garden, enjoying the variety of flowers with their glorious colors. They reminded me of Your matchless creativity and infinite beauty. What a wonder!

In response to this fleeting appreciation, You appeared before me with a smile of good humor. Being everywhere, You can manifest anywhere, although it may seem as if You come from nowhere! I was so stunned that I greeted You with an awed and grateful silence.

Before I could recover from this unexpected heavenly surprise, You asked me casually, "How are you?"

"I'm okay," I replied vaguely, still under the spell of Your arrival.

You looked probingly at me. "Really?"

I felt my mood shift, and answered somewhat defensively. "Why? Don't you think so?"

"But are you at peace with yourself?" You asked gently.

Your loving concern disarmed me completely, and gave me the courage to open my wounded heart. "In fact, my mind is in shambles, and my peace is in pieces!" I confessed.

"Yet you look quite composed," You observed.

"That is only camouflage," I answered.

You nodded, as though in sympathy. "I'm glad you say so. Generally, people do camouflage themselves, especially when they are at parties and public gatherings."

"But aren't these occasions supposed to be times for relaxation and relief from the stress of life?"

"Yes, but you soon find that all this merriment is only temporary. By the time you reach home, you begin to brood on unpleasant events connected with some of the persons you have had conversations with."

"You're right," I admitted. "Even when I open certain letters, the contents irritate me. Or when I occasionally hear comments made during the day that I disagree with, I feel aggravated. I often lose my mental balance as a result. How can I get over this?"

"Don't lose heart, and you will receive My help," You assured me.

"But what is the real cause of all this annoyance and irritation?" I asked.

"It is natural that many unexpected things happen to you which annoy you, and this creates a sense of frustration.

Sometimes you cannot help but express your irritation outwardly. But the more you see your life as being harmoniously interwoven with those you meet, your responses will be less selfish and more loving. The truth is, meeting others is really a meeting with your own many selves, in order that you may eventually find your real Self in Me. When you begin to feel My presence in others, then the qualities that you envy in them will exude a new perfume of appreciation for you. Discovering My presence in others is always a joyous surprise, and goes a long way toward helping Me to help you."

"You are right," I acknowledged. "I have experienced this. But then I totally forget the blessings You have showered on me, and I continue the bad habit of keeping a careful count of all my troubles. This seems to be deeply ingrained in me."

"That is because you forget that delightful encounters are waiting for you just around the corner."

"Are they?"

"Yes, because life is always moving, consciously or unconsciously, toward that Bliss which is your Real Nature."

"Yet it seems that in spite of anticipating this Bliss, I am constantly passing through disturbing experiences."

Again, I saw a look of deep sympathy in Your eyes. "The disturbances you speak of are always relative to your acceptance of My will. If you take the things that happen to you as expressions of My will, you will feel less annoyed, and the spirit of acceptance will be awakened in you. Learn to accept life as it is, without getting annoyed, and I will help you. Do you think that I am cruel?"

I could only look at You.

You shook Your head solemnly. "No. Even if I wished to be, I could not. I love you. I love all."

I was greatly moved and had no idea of what to say. "You know that I am an ordinary person," I floundered. "I can't understand everything You have tried to convey to me during Your visits, yet I am more grateful to You than I can say."

Your eyes sparkled merrily. "Right," You agreed. "This is all so simple, yet for you, not-so-simple. I will tell you a secret! The jug of My intoxicating wine does not notice when the cup runs over. This is my weakness, that I continue to share beyond your capacity."

You smiled benignly. "If you ever desire to take a life journey with Me, you will pass through exciting and challenging events that will bring you moments of joy and agony never experienced before. These experiences will nourish your spirit to continue the journey onward. But the first step is the real adventure."

Your words set my heart aflutter. "Will you help me to take that step?"

"That is totally dependent on your wish and will, for whatever is imposed does not last long. But perhaps, because you are asking this of Me sincerely, you have already sown the seed for such a journey."

"Will I have to wait long before it begins?"

You cautioned, "Well, this step requires a brave heart. You have to be ready to suffer with joyous resignation to My will. But don't worry about the delay. Have you ever watched the slow, graceful rising of the sun? Or thought about the gradual ripening of a fruit nestled among the leaves of a tree? Or the unfolding of a flower bud to the light of the day? There is joy in waiting and longing for the manifestation of My greater presence within you."

"Will I then be at peace with myself?" I questioned.

"Only when your mind and heart realize that the real rest lies in My constant companionship."

"Although this has answered my question, it does not provide a solution."

"Here is a simple clue: try to think of Me more and more wholeheartedly."

"You often ask me to remember You, but what is the name by which You most like to be remembered?"

"Any name that naturally comes from the depths of your heart is My name. The language of the heart blooms from My Silence, which speaks through all languages, but is bound by none."

With humble reverence, I quipped affectionately, "In Your omniscience You commit to nothing; in Your omnipotence You get bound by anything, or by any word."

You gave me a heart-penetrating look, then rose to Your feet. "All right, then, I'm leaving."

In silence, we moved slowly to the side gate of the garden and parted. It was a sad parting, though in some way not painful. Yet I could not stop the tears from rolling down my cheeks. They were tears of an unspeakable relief and joy.

You had gone a few steps, then turned and cast a most intimate glance at me. Then it was as though You disappeared into the shimmering rays of the morning, into the glistening grass, the flowers, and everything under the blue dome of the sky. But that brief glance lit a tiny flame of Your luminous presence in my heart. It felt so pure, so tender, that I feared the slightest doubt about Your visit might extinguish it.

> Oh Compassionate Father!
> Let this slender flame continue to glow
> and guide my every step to You —
> the Light that is ever shining within!

What Is Weakness? What Is Strength?

I was feeling low and forlorn, as if I were all alone in an alien land. So burdensome was this weight of despair that when You suddenly appeared before me, instead of being delighted in Your presence, I blurted out:

"Oh, why must I feel so weak and alone?"

With a compassionate yet slightly mischievous smile You answered, "Because this is helping you to establish inner communion with Me. Tell Me the truth — how often do you remember Me when you are physically fit?"

"To be honest, not often. But can't You give me both strength and the capacity to remember You at the same time?" I argued.

"Of course," You replied with calm assurance. "Nothing is impossible for Me."

"Then why don't You?"

"That is My weakness."

"Weakness? How can the Omnipotent One have a weakness? This is news to me!" I exclaimed, surprised.

"There is a reason for it," You assured me. "My weakness gives your heart strength."

"How? I am not following You."

"Metal is put into a fire to temper it, then the blacksmith rains blows on it with his hammer. Why? So that the metal will become stronger and able to withstand hard use for a long time without breaking. Aren't you wishing for everlasting joy?"

"Yes, I am. That is what I long for most."

"To ensure everlasting joy, you must pass through weakness, nervousness, doubt, despair, and the like. However, My compassion is such that even extreme weakness serves to nurture the seed of strength buried in your heart. At the opportune time that seed will suddenly blossom, and you will be surprised at the results.

"So don't worry about your weaknesses, keep up a cheerful front, and you will be able to witness My love for you in a variety of ways."

This answer consoled my heart, but I couldn't refrain from quipping, "It seems to me that You work better with the weaknesses of people than You do with their strengths!"

You smiled delightedly at this and asked me, "Is that My weakness or My strength?"

I kept silent.

Lost Opportunity

Sitting on a large rock by the lake's edge, I was looking out into the depth of the night sky. The water was ever-so-softly lapping at the shore. The vast glassy surface of the lake, reflecting the myriad stars above, was perfectly still. Watching this exquisite sight, I experienced a profound sense of peace.

Then a strong breeze began to rustle through the nearby pines. As the wind moved across the lake, waves began to ripple along the surface. The starlit portrait, which had been mirrored with such transparent clarity, was suddenly dashed into patterns of diffused light lost in the waves. As this happened, the peacefulness of my mind also gave way to a frenzy of scattered thoughts.

The startling contrast of the two scenes I witnessed left me unsettled. Gradually the wind calmed down and the water's surface again became placid.

I heard familiar footsteps behind me, and You came and

sat by my side. Though I was happy to see You, instead of greeting You, I exclaimed, "What a beautiful scene You just missed! You came a little late."

"I am never late nor early; I always know the right moment," You answered.

"You are the Perfectionist who conserves His omnipresence only to release it at the opportune moment."

"But what did I miss? What was it that captivated you so much?" You asked.

Feeling a bit confused, I found myself stammering. "Well, I don't know which affected me more, the charming settled reflections of the stars on the still surface of the lake, or the shimmering of their subsequent diffused patterns. It is hard for me to express!"

"What do you really wish to convey?" You asked gently.

"That's what is difficult. Trying to describe it all only reminds me of one of my most chronic problems. I am often indecisive and frustrated about how to adequately express myself in words. I try to choose the right words, but I am hardly ever satisfied. And this seems to result in an uncertainty of actions."

You were silent for some moments, then gave me a penetrating, serious look. "Unless and until you sincerely try to detach yourself from the *many* by which you are surrounded, you cannot become attached to the One in all. In your daily living, you are distracted by that which is impermanent, whether it be the steady or shattered reflections of the stars. And you forget the ever-renewing Spirit that is ever-alive in everything, everywhere. If you try to remember this ever-renewing Spirit, you will be less likely to be overpowered by the passing events of your daily life. For this, your longing to live in My presence has to be rooted more and more in your awareness of My companionship."

Your loving words deeply touched my heart. Seeing this, You looked pleased and continued, "When you think that no one sees you, I, the One, am diligently watching you. When you feel that no one hears you, I, the One, am listening intently to you. Because you are Mine, I am the One who is most intimately concerned about you."

How long we talked after that, and what diverse subjects we covered, I don't remember. But gradually I became aware that the crescent moon had risen high in the sky. The still surface of the water reflected the beauty of the crescent rising overhead. As before, I became deeply engrossed in the splendor of this vision, and my attention was totally diverted from You, the "full moon," sitting by my side.

Some moments later I realized my mistake, but as I turned to You, I found You were gone. I felt bitterly ashamed, but it was too late. In Your presence, the slightest distraction is a lost opportunity!

Yet in spite of such failures, You continue to bless me with Your visits. What an unconditional compassion You have. In these visits Your radiant presence fills my being with indescribable raptures. Your loving words are carved into my heart, but how quickly they seem to fade!

As I gazed at the clear lake, the reflections of the stars and the crescent no longer held any charm for me. Instead, tears of repentance welled in my eyes. They awakened in me an intense, deep longing for Your next visit. When shall that be?

You alone know.

Attention and Recognition

I was attending a concert, listening to a famous group of musicians and enjoying their singing. Though I had come a bit late to the program, I observed that many people I knew were present. However, when it was over, no one seemed to have taken notice of my arrival, not even my close friends. Perhaps they were overwhelmed by the presentation of such beautiful music. I had also been touched by the performance, but somewhere within me I felt hurt, feeling that I had been neglected by my friends. I expected at least a little attention from someone.

That night I slept well. However, when I awoke, the nightmare of feeling totally neglected at the gathering the previous evening was still hovering over me. While attending to the morning chores, I felt uneasy and was not in a good mood at all. I knew that I was harboring ill feelings from last night, but I could not let go of them.

Naturally, I thought of You, but did not expect You to visit me. However, in Your omniscience and unconditional intimacy, You walked straight into my room. Instead of looking radiant, You appeared worried and asked me with concern, "What's the matter? What's wrong with you?"

"I feel a bit out of sorts," I admitted sheepishly.

"Why? What happened?"

Somewhat awkwardly I explained, "At a musical performance I attended last night, none of my friends acknowledged me. I felt neglected, hurt, and lonely."

Some silent moments ticked away before You gently spoke. "The main cause of this is that you feel yourself to be a person who, because of age, position, or talent, has some special rights over others. You want them to pay attention to you. But in fact, you have to be more careful, more watchful, when others praise and respect you, because through such appreciation your ego-centered life is strengthened."

"I see." I swallowed with difficulty.

You continued, "You like yourself to be treated as some-one special, but you should be ready to accept what others take you to be. Think of My love, which is equally for all; it has no preferences. A wildflower in a meadow and a beautiful rose in a garden have the same exposure to the sunlight above and the touch of the ground below."

"What can I do differently?" I asked humbly.

"Though beyond time, I am the One who is close to you,

in and through each breath. This is the mystery in the time-bound Creation that reveals My sense of humor. However, beginning to experience the bliss in My remembrance as you breathe or move about can help free you from the grip of pride and the expectation of special attention from others. When you remember Me, you gradually begin to forget the ego-centered life. With My remembrance, you will develop appreciation for the various aspects of life without any personal attachment to them. For this, let the practice of offering these attachments to Me awaken within you."

"How does this come about?"

"Offering begins to germinate and blossom by getting off the ring that binds you. This will in its course relieve you from expecting special attention from others. As a result, the raising up and dashing down of your spirit for not being recognized will begin to lessen."

"Listening to You makes me aware of my imperfections, and I feel that to become aware of Your love within me I need to traverse a different dimension. To me, this is like walking on a delicate thread, finer and more fragile than silk, sustained and guided only by Your grace. To remember You wholeheartedly," I acknowledged gratefully, "is to imbibe trust in You and to inherit the courage to go on."

"Yes," You nodded. "Then you will begin to realize that you are not someone special, and that I love all. This will gradually transform your inner life, and you shall be more and more tolerant and unmindful of whether others pay attention to you or not. Desire for attention solicits recognition, and if it is not received, this results in tension. Why not accept these happenings as My wish rather than clinging to the responses you expect from others?"

"This seems very difficult," I responded.

"True. It is a process where you stumble and fall and rise again. At each step you have to see with the eyes of the heart and the sight of faith. If you lean on Me as completely as you can, the doors to My presence will open up to you. For instance, when you enter any place, whether a drawing room or a dining room, a store or a restaurant, if you treat that space as a part of My mansion, then you will find it filled with My presence. With your focus on Me, you yourself will find other ways leading to the unwavering sublime experience of companionship with Me."

"In my relationship with You, I become aware of so many imperfections," I lamented.

You smiled. "I want your imperfections. Continue to offer them to Me without hesitation, for I am Perfection personified."

I had no idea that the so-called social conventions of life, such as whether or not one is greeted, had such a tight grip over my life. But in Your matchless way, You made me aware of such bindings and imperfections. I hope Your gift of remembrance shall, slowly but surely, wipe clear the slate of my heart. This was a wonderful revelation to me that You use my mistakes and misunderstandings as opportunities to offer the right perspectives toward life.

You left — but your profound, heart-warming words were afloat and ringing within me. And like the melodies of the temple bells, they were chanting inspiring tunes in my heart. May these help me to lead a life that shall please You.

A Pleasantry

You were sitting beside me on my bed; I was immensely thrilled. Your presence drenched me with a feeling of such relaxation that I felt I could freely converse with You on any subject without the least hesitation.

That morning I had taken a long walk and watched the glory of the rising sun — the endless rays of light stretching across the horizon. I have often felt as though the sky overhead were calling out to me, "Find out what I really am!"

I found You in a delightful mood, so I thought it was the right time to open up the "sky-high" subject, not as a problem needing a solution, but just as a point of inquiry. I said, "What is space? I have often asked this question of myself with no satisfying answer."

You looked amused and, instead of giving me a reply, posed a counterquestion: "What is time? Do you pass time or do you pass in and through time?"

"I don't know. I cannot even guess, although I am in it all the time, not knowing what it is," I replied.

"Then how will you understand what space is, even though you are surrounded by it all the time? Space and time are like twins. So aren't these questions bigger than life?"

"I admit that, but do You want me to suppress such inquiries? Whenever I move, I am under the sky and moving through time. Am I not?"

"Yes, you are."

"Then do You expect me to stop trying to find out what they are? If You were to provide me with some clue, it might make me aware of the scope of my inability to understand."

"Okay. If you are going to take this as a game, keep an open mind and remember that space is a boundless cage for the entire Creation."

Your statements threw me off and helped me to realize the folly of trying to touch the moon with my hands. So I joked, "With the myriad stars, the Creation in space reminds me of an infinitely enormous cake!"

You quipped back, "And you devour this whole cake when you are in deep sleep!"

"And I swallow time too," I added. And we both laughed. "But the irony is that when I get up, this cake becomes like a hard round rock candy which I can neither break nor swallow. But may I ask You one more question?"

"Why one? Ask as many as you wish."

"Just one. . . . Tell me, where are You when I am in deep sleep?"

"I play the part of the watchman who wakes you at the appointed time." There was a mischievous smile on Your face.

"How nice it would be if You were not to wake me up at all."

"I cannot do that because you will accuse me of suppressing your desire to know the realities of time and space," You replied, winking at me.

"Well, I give up," I said.

"So you say. But your thoughts on these two unfathomable subjects are deeply rooted within your mind and heart."

"When will these thoughts be wiped out?" I asked eagerly.

"Don't be impatient. There will be the moment out of time, so to speak, when this game in time and space will be over and you shall abide in Eternal Wakefulness, which is timeless and spaceless."

Overwhelmed by Your assurances, I looked at You in amazement . . .

Just then I heard the ring of the door bell — waking me up from my dream. That day after a long walk I had felt a bit tired, so, resting on the bed, I had dozed off. My friend had come at the appointed time. As I went to open the door, a new question popped up in my mind: "How are time and space in the dream state related to my waking state?"

Anyway, meeting You, even in a dream is matchless fun, a marvelous pleasantry.

Playing One's Part

I was resting in my room on a comfortable reclining chair. However, my mind was restless, unsettled like a scrambled egg. I was deeply disturbed by the current social order, where higher human values were being ruthlessly trampled. Such attitudes of people not only irritated me emotionally, but also affected my physical health. I was feeling depressed and weak.

While I was deeply absorbed in such thoughts, most unexpectedly, as though by magic, the room was transformed into a vast ocean. Sometimes the water looked dark, dirty, and turbulent, with frothing waves cresting high; while at other times its surface barely rippled, glimmering with charming shades of blue and green. It was incredible.

Then, as if this were not frightening enough, suddenly I saw a big ball of light emerge from the ocean and soar into the sky. As it was rising higher and higher, innumerable little drops of light streaked downward. I gazed at it in astonishment, when suddenly the ball stopped rising and plummeted into the ocean with a gigantic splash. In the next instant the entire ocean was aflame.

I was overwhelmed, but before I could disengage my mind from these successive stunning events, the entire vision completely vanished and was replaced with a deep and total darkness. This transformation calmed me down a bit, and I felt relieved. A sense of peace fell over me. Thank heavens!

Just then, from the seemingly limitless darkness, I saw You, encircled in a glorious soft light, taking long strides toward me. Before I knew it, You were sitting facing me.

With a benign freshness gleaming in Your eyes, You gently remarked, "You look frightened, astounded. What's happened to you?"

Still under the awesome influence of the earlier vision, all I could say was, "Nothing!"

"If 'nothing' can make you look so apprehensive, what would you look like if 'something' happened?" You flashed a marvelous, intimate smile that had such a soothing effect on me that it brought me back to my normal state.

Immediately I blurted out, "What was that strange vision I just had?"

You seemed to know all about it and replied, "It was all projected from the depths of your mind, through a pinhole point of time, and then it receded back."

"But why should this occur?"

"Nothing happens by accident. Whatever occurs is part of a greater design in a person's life. The vision you had was a natural unfolding meant to shake you and wake you from your present awareness. Sometimes, when you are deeply affected, interior regions of the mind project symbolic patterns. However, if one is connected with Me, such glimpses lighten and transform the inner life."

"What is the meaning of these symbolic patterns?" I asked.

"Your life is a sequence of events and experiences which inwardly form patterns and images into symbols. When you are deeply affected, such as by the attitudes of others, these symbols are energized and projected onto the screen of your awareness. However, for those who get connected with Me, the Source of all, these symbolic patterns begin to dissolve, thereby eliminating a load of impressions and making your life light and lively."

"I am too short-sighted to even begin to glimpse Your vast horizons. So could You just shed enough light for my next few steps? For instance, why should I feel so dejected and be affected so much by the unsympathetic attitudes of other people?"

"It is not just you who feel this way; there are many others, though the intensity of their feelings may vary. These feelings arise from sympathy and concern for others. They are good, a sign that love is alive in the heart. However, each one should try to become more aware of the nature of their responses. Shouldn't you too?"

"How?"

"Sensitivity to human suffering and the desire to help those who suffer are definitely commendable, but you should not be so carried away by your concern that you make yourself miserable. Your dis-ease with suffering can become a kind of disease."

"Disease? Then I would like to know its symptoms, its nature, so that I can be cured!" I exclaimed.

"You unnecessarily try to decide what others should do and unduly react if they fail to do it. In fact, these are their problems, but you begin to own them as yours. To render effective assistance, first you have to find out your own capacities and capabilities."

"You expect me to know my physical ability and mental capacities?"

"Yes. Instead of trying to change the world, you have to change yourself."

"By first understanding my own nature?" I asked. "Then I find my niche?"

"Right. Then your response to suffering will be more practical." You added reassuringly, "You will also feel My help in playing your part with a cheerful heart. Then, while relating to the world, you will be pleasing Me and gradually coming closer to Me."

"I would like to make the world a happier place."

You looked happy at this simple sentiment and remarked,

"That is good. Do your best, and I will see to the rest. And do not worry; remain bright and cheerful."

My spirit smiled and my heart rejoiced at Your encouragement. Your words enthralled my heart, and its hunger to continue listening to You grew more intense. Overwhelmed at the profound depths of Your simple, loving responses, I looked at Your radiant face and Your eyes full of love and compassion. I was still bathing in the incredible beauty of Your presence when You departed as quietly and quickly as You had appeared.

The next moment I was aware of being alone in the room. I had wanted to communicate my warm-hearted gratitude to You for coming to me, but my lips had been sealed. A few tears rolled down my cheeks. The language of love is tears and silence.

Your visit uplifted me. Your grace can turn a stone into an angel and poison into nectar. This is the magic of Your unconditional compassion and concern: that You stoop down to anyone's level. I silently invoked You within my heart. "O Glorious One, now let Your loving remembrance flow through the veins of my spirit so that its purity shall guide me to offer all my movements, thoughts, and feelings as my love offerings to You."

In a happy mood, I got up from my chair and wrote a letter to a retirement home, expressing my willingness to volunteer for a few hours each weekend. I also made out a check in the name of a charitable relief organization. Then I went into the garden and watered the plants and picked some beautiful flowers for a bouquet. I intended to present this bouquet to my neighbor's little daughter. As I held it in my hand, I envisioned her sparkling eyes and her smile of innocent joy. In these ways, I felt I had played my part, according to my capabilities, leaving the larger results to You, and that these three acts were my loving contributions of body, mind, and heart. In Your infinite Game there is no such thing as small or great. Your love can mirror through any response or any other thing.

Selfishness, Selflessness, and the "Real I"

It was nighttime. I had just finished arranging the covers about me when You quietly entered the room and sat on the edge of my bed. I was filled with happiness that You had come.

We talked together about many things — about the latest sports news, the weather, my health. I had just discovered a new flavor of ice cream that day that I especially liked and I told you all about it. You smiled in appreciation, as if You also would have liked to have had some. I told You a few jokes and together we laughed. Once again I was a little surprised at how interested You were in even the most mundane or seemingly trivial facets of life. I was moved by the way You treat life as a whole, not dividing it into important and unimportant aspects.

Then You became quiet and I noticed a peaceful hush pervading the dimly lit room. Wistfully, You looked out my window at the twinkling stars scattered across the night sky. A gentle breeze moved the tops of the trees, their dancing branches silhouetted against the faint rays of the stars.

You said, "Is it time for you to go to sleep?"

As I thought of ways to keep You with me a little longer, I remembered that for the past two or three nights I had not slept well.

"Can I ask You a favor?" I ventured shyly.

Your receptive silence enfolded me.

"Will You bless me with sound sleep tonight?"

"Why not?" You answered.

"But isn't it selfish of me to ask this of You?"

"How so? You want sound sleep so that when you wake up in the morning, you may try to be more aware of Me. Isn't that right?"

"True, but won't this asking only nurture my attitude of selfishness, which may keep me away from You?"

You closed Your eyes as if in concentration. Tranquillity filled the room. "Yes, in a way. For instance, do you remember that particular flavor of ice cream you were telling Me about?"

"Yes," I replied happily. "I enjoyed it very much."

"But you forgot Me while you were relishing it, didn't you?"

What You said was right. I kept a shamed silence.

You appeared not to notice my reaction, but continued, Your voice sweet, "But if, while enjoying your dinner, you think about Me in a natural way, you will still be able to enjoy the various tastes. In fact, you may find even more pleasure in them because you will be sharing them with Me, making Me your companion, offering Me each sip and taste. The difference will be that you will still relish, but not crave."

"What do You mean by this?" I had quickly forgotten my embarrassment.

"Normally, if you like what you eat, you crave more. If you share it with Me, you will still enjoy it but will be much less caught up in the pleasure."

My heart was soothed by this, but not my mind. "You say that I will still find pleasure in my dinner. But isn't this selfish?"

Not the least impatient with my probing, You used another example to illustrate Your point. "When you earn money, not just to fulfill your own desires, but for the happiness and well-being of others, gradually your motivation, even if it began as a mixed one, will change. It will become more selfless."

Intellectually, I understood what You were saying. Still, I doubted whether I would ever be able to lose my strong sense of self. "Even though I am earning for others as well, won't 'I' be doing it?" I asked plaintively. "My sense of 'I' will remain, and whatever I do will be done with some degree of selfishness."

"And why do you fear selfishness? 'I-ness' is in both selfishness and selflessness, but selfishness is more binding than selflessness. As long as you are alive, how can you ever be without a self? This 'I-ness' of the self is the innate desire for survival as a separate entity. It is the root of selfishness in each one."

"So what does this all mean?" I asked, taken aback by Your response. "Where does it all lead?"

Smiling reassuringly, You replied, "The more the root of 'I-ness' begins to dry, the more selflessness begins to blossom. And when this root is totally dried out, the 'Real I-ness' of My existence prevails. That will be the ending of selfishness and selflessness, and the emergence of the 'Real I' that I am."

My look of hopeful questioning entreated You to continue.

"The only way out is to purify your 'I-ness' with My remembrance. Thoughts of Me will gradually clean the mirror of your life, allowing it to reflect more and more of My presence. If you let Me into your heart, the knots of selfishness will be untied. Gradually, selflessness will lead you to find the Self-in-all, wherein you feel My presence more intimately."

I was overwhelmed by Your compassionate words, by Your beauty, Your mercy, and by the fact that You are always there waiting; waiting, without imposing Yourself, while it is I who turn You away. A grateful peace washed over me, and the quiet remained unbroken for some time.

Then, with a voice gentle with motherly love, You said, "Feel free with Me. Don't hesitate to call on Me for anything,

anything at all — I know what to give and what not to give."

Consoled by Your compassion, I assumed my usual child-like manner with You. Without thinking, I blurted out, "If You don't appear in my dreams, it's okay. But don't let nasty things disturb my sleep."

"If you think of Me before going to sleep, it will unwind the worries of the day, and I will take charge of your dreams."

"So would it be good for me to think of You for some time before going to bed?"

"Yes, and . . ."

"And also when I wake up?" I suggested, not letting You finish Your sentence.

You showed Your appreciation for my enthusiasm with a smile. Gently You repeated. "As you live in My remembrance, there will be less and less selfishness. Eventually, as My Grace washes over you, the 'Real I' shall emerge."

Your expression was so loving, so affectionate, that I found myself asking, "When do You sleep?"

Again You smiled and then said, "Sleep always remains wide awake in Me."

This cryptic reply, I knew, was beyond my understanding, and I remained silent.

But such thoughts were swept away by the sweet look You gave me as you said, "Good night, sweet dreams." And then You left.

As I pulled the sheet over me, I marveled at the way You

are able to stoop to my level, share my interests, and yet imbue our conversations with Your inimitable sense of humor and loving patience.

I did sleep well that night.

The Universal Life

A lone star shone in the immense darkness. It seemed to reflect my own state — a pinprick of wavering light surrounded by a dense, engulfing depression. Suddenly I heard You say, "The root cause of all your problems is your identification with them."

"I understand that," I said, "at least in theory. And sometimes I even feel the reality of it."

"But what you should really understand is that My visits to you are meant to shake you loose from the grip of self-identification."

I tried to sound consoled: "Well, at least that's something."

You laughed as though I'd cracked a splendid joke. "My dear fellow, it's not just 'something,' it is *the* thing which all beings consciously or unconsciously long for! But to derive any real benefit, one has to have a *live heart*."

"*Live heart?*" I responded. "I haven't heard that expression, though I've read in spiritual literature about something called 'the eye of the heart.'"

"Yes, and also wide-open eyes and sharp ears too! It is essential that you develop a sensitive and discriminating awareness of your life."

I was beginning to feel exasperated, not by Your words, but by my own inability to make practical use of them.

"Listen carefully," You said, disarming me with Your smile. "As you gain this awareness, pressure becomes pleasure, and your plight a delight. That which oppresses you will begin to amuse you. All that is required of you is that you remember Me in the midst of both your joys and trials. As soon as you do this, you will notice 'happenings' that reveal My presence and My help. These are never lacking, but you tend to forget them when your circumstances change. So in addition to developing eyes and ears, you have to open up to the latent, potent flow of My presence within you.

"It is true," I acknowledged, "that whenever I have called on You, You have never been absent from me. Why is it so difficult for me to remember this, and so easy to forget?"

"In the beginning, it requires a sort of repetition," You said, reassuringly, "like taking a bath. The effects of soap and water last only for a time; the same is true of your experiences of My presence, at least in terms of your conscious awareness. Therefore, you have to continue to bathe in the stream of My presence by focusing on Me. I reside within you as the ever-fresh spring of all blessedness. Feel My loving presence enveloping you, supporting you, protecting you."

Your words moved me deeply. "But how am I to do this? How am I to develop this awareness?"

"Practice it, and gradually, it will blossom into a graceful art. In a most natural way, you will find all your thoughts and feelings grounded in My unbinding love, and the ties of your self-identification, the endless web you have woven, will be loosened."

"I have grave doubts about how well I will succeed in this," I confessed, reflecting on past failures.

"Don't begin with doubts and negativity, but with trust and confidence in Me. Do you think I won't help you?" But then You cautioned, "You must also put forth your earnest efforts, and not waste time worrying about your failures."

I saw a faraway look in Your eyes, and there was a deep feeling of serenity about You. On previous occasions, I had noticed that this was a sign that You were in a mood to probe into some inner mystery of life.

"My Infinity is absolutely free and purposeless, yet, within the domain of creation, there is not a single happening that is without significance. No doubt it is often difficult for the ordinary intellect to understand the laws which express My compassion. The unfathomable Game of My unfettered Universal Life — a Game engendered by Me — is played out within the expanse of My Being, and returns to Me in the end."

You paused, drawing in Your breath. You ran Your fingers through Your hair and then covered Your face with Your hands. It seemed You wanted to hide Your radiance, yet I noticed a golden glow encircling You. I was lost in wonder. And then, with a look of fathomless love, You resumed:

"You see, the blossoming of a delicate primrose and the force of a devastating earthquake, the eruption of a catastrophic volcano and the shimmering of a cool beam of moonlight — each of these is the result of innumerable interrelated laws. However, actions and reactions are affected on the human level by free will. For with the formation of conscious individuality, everyone has the privilege of setting sail in various directions on the uncharted oceans of life. This individuality and the oceans it explores are illusory.

"In truth, there is only one infinite Ocean, and all the innumerable finite drops of individuality are only appearances. The drops vibrate with self-assertion, setting forth ripples and waves. Until the waves cease and the vibrations are stilled, the *Oceanity* of the real Ocean cannot be experienced. Until then, the interplay of countless laws on numberless levels of existence within My Universal Life continues. It is unfathomable! Incomprehensible! Yet, see the wonder — in every individual activity, great or small, My Game is reflected, as the sun is reflected in the smallest drop. The macrocosm is in each microcosm; in the same way, My nonbinding love is latent within everyone all the time."

Reeling from the enormity of Your Game, my heart quaked and my mind floundered. This was truly beyond me. Yet a strange peace settled over me. "Yes, it is much more than I can imagine. The mystery of Your Universal Life is higher than the highest heavens."

You nodded, with a glance of fatherly affection. "Yes, higher than the highest, yet closer than the closest. So don't be amazed, or become dazed. Be courageous. Know Me as the most intimate One residing within you, and follow the way that your heart honestly leads you."

At that moment Your face lit up with the innocence of a child, and I asked myself, "Is this the same One who, only a moment ago, was making the most profound declarations?" And I entreated You, "Please pour Your life-giving presence into every moment of my life. This will be a blessed gift from You which will ultimately dissolve me in Your Ocean."

Your smile burst forth like the radiance of the morning sun; every part of my being was touched by its warmth. Overwhelmed, I closed my eyes, lowered my head, and — amazingly — I began to hear Your voice within me, as though with the ears of the heart:

> At any time, whatever you may be doing, come
> outside of yourself and call on Me; invite Me to

join you, and I will be participating in even the
smallest of your activities. In reality, it is I who
maintain and sustain you, but you know it not.
Don't worry, just remember that I am anxious to
help you, yet I do not wish to impose anything
upon you. I am most impatient to free you from
your self-created web of falseness. I am the
Ocean of Love, Love that is all-powerful yet
infinitely helpless. This is the delight, and the
plight of My Universal Life.

The flow of communication stopped, and I was drowned
in Your luminous silence. I do not know how long I remained
in this state, but at last, gazing up again at the distant star, I
saw You there smiling at me, Your eyes gleaming with gaiety.
I raised my hands to the heavens and heartily invoked
You:

> Let Your remembrance,
> Your Name, be my only Song,
> tuning me to sing the glory
> of Your Universal Life.

Since that night a new dawn has broken on the horizon
of my relationship with You.

A Wonderful Bath!

Standing by the dresser after my bath, I sprinkled a little cologne on my collar as usual. As I placed the bottle on the table, I heard Your loving voice: "Nice cologne!"

Taken aback by this sweet surprise, I gazed at Your resplendent form. "No fragrance can excel the perfume of Your presence."

You laughed gently at this, and we both settled into chairs.

"It seems you had a very good bath," You observed.

"Yes, very refreshing. First I showered, the cooling water energizing me, then I got into the tub. Water, water, what a great blessing!"

"In the tub, did you just rub and scrub your body and cleanse the pores?" You asked.

"Of course. What else am I supposed to do?" I wondered.

"Bathing time is a good time for song and sermon."

"I do sing sometimes," I replied, "but what do You mean by 'sermon'?"

"Bathing is a time when you are alone, with no one watching you and no one present to preach to you. It offers you the opportunity to listen to the silent wisdom of the body. It is an occasion for you to discover the mysteries hidden under your skin."

"I'm afraid I don't follow you," I had to admit.

"In a way it is simple. As you scrub the skin, why not think of the muscles and tendons underneath, which make movement possible? Think of the arteries, filled with different types of blood cells bringing nourishment to your body; reflect on the countless nerves which give you the sense of touch and feeling. If you do this, your earlier approach to bathing as a routine chore will be slowly washed away. It will completely change the way you think of your body. You will begin to marvel at it. The functioning of the body is such that even a single hair serves a purpose and helps sustain you. Gradually, as you become more aware, the beauty and sanctity of each part of your body will be revealed."

"I am really eager to hear more on this subject!"

You looked pleased by my enthusiasm. "Today I will just give you an elementary introduction."

"That would be most appropriate for a person like me," I acknowledged.

"Good that you know your limits. Now, listen. You have

had this body for years, but tell me, how many times have you seriously thought about the specific working of any part, large or small?"

My wordless stare showed that I hadn't ever given any real thought to the subject.

You smiled and continued. "Don't worry. I don't expect you to start studying subjects like anatomy and physiology, psychology, and the like."

"Thank goodness," I sighed. "Those subjects are far beyond my grasp."

"Right. For now, as a first step, why not start by trying to be mindful of the connections between your body and its workings, and your thoughts and feelings? If you do this, you will begin to be aware of the degree of your attachment and close identification with the body. In fact, your wonderful body of flesh is a captivating cage made of sense pleasures. Through a process of silently witnessing the complex functions and reactions of the body, you will become more and more conscious of it. This shall be your 'lifeline'; it will cleanse your mind and purify your heart, and help to unfetter you from the attachments of the body."

"A kind of bathing in Your pure being," I said in wonderment.

"Yes. My companionship throughout your daily life will free you from the limiting cage of sense pleasures."

After saying this, You kept silent and appeared very

peaceful. Your words seemed to penetrate deeply through my skin and circulate through my entire being. I knew I was tightly caught up in the den of 'I-den-tification,' and there seemed to be no way to come out of it.

Sensing my predicament, You lightened the mood by asking me, "Have you ever carefully looked at your earlobes, the tip of your nose, or your own eyes?"

These simple questions brought me down to earth as if from a great height. But instead of looking in the mirror to see my earlobes, I looked straight into Your eyes. To my astonishment, I saw two beams of glorious light stretching back to a measureless distance. Awed, I withdrew my sight, then sheepishly looked in the mirror and began to feel the tip of my nose.

You smiled, and Your amusement relieved me of my embarrassment. "I don't wish to bother you with this topic anymore. I hope I haven't kept you from your breakfast."

Perhaps You were looking for an excuse to leave, and Your sense of humor provided it. You put the bottle of cologne back in its case. There was a twinkle in Your eye, and I felt as if You were bathing me with a most delightful perfume. In Your company every moment is fragrant with the glorious purity of Your presence.

I was having my first real bath that day, a matchless introduction to the treasure of being mindful of the mysteries within the body!

Seeking Happiness

The horizon was calling out for light. Slowly the pink hues of dawn spread across the sky, and then the golden rays of the sun began to stream through the leaves of the trees. The branches stirred and danced above me in the fragrant breeze, crimson blossoms smiling joyously. Beneath this delightful canopy in the garden, I found myself in that blissful atmosphere, sitting next to You on a bench.

Neither of us spoke for quite some time. Then I said, "How happy I am to find You here. What has brought You here this morning?"

You made a casual gesture. "The wind is free and blows where it wishes," You answered. "I don't need a reason for visiting someone. By the way, tell me, what is on your mind just now?"

"Just now?" I reflected momentarily, to crystallize the thoughts and feelings that I had been experiencing since I'd gotten up that morning. "Actually, it is on my mind that I want to be happy, that's all. I have a strong feeling that I should seek, and continue to seek, everlasting happiness."

"And why do you want to be happy?" You asked, with a smile.

"I don't know. It just seems natural."

"Why don't you try to find the reason?"

"Is there something wrong in wanting to be happy?" I said, feeling defensive.

You laughed softly. "Did I say there was something wrong? I only asked you to try to find the source of this longing."

I was reassured. "Well, all right, let me think. . . . When I got up this morning, after having a very deep and sound sleep, I felt so rested and peaceful and full of joy that now I find myself wishing that this state would continue in me forever."

"And what has stopped it? Why didn't you just remain in your sound sleep?"

"How wonderful if that were possible! But every day, somehow I always wake up, whether I sleep soundly or fitfully. Why is that?"

"You yourself are the reason," You disclosed, smiling again.

"I'm afraid I don't follow You," I confessed.

"Even during the period of deep sleep, dormant within you are the impulses to experience the various sense pleasures that you are attached to. Also latent within are the feelings of anger, lust, jealousy, envy. . . . These shake you and wake you from your sleep."

"Yes, that is the problem," I agreed. "But how am I to solve it?"

"By not treating it as a problem." You chuckled. "When you are awake, you simply but sincerely try to be aware that I am the Source of bliss within you. This will lighten the burden of the 'I'-centered actions, thoughts, and feelings that enmesh you. And if you do this, you may find yourself experiencing a deeper peace and equanimity during your waking life."

"Is it really so simple?" I wondered. "Normally, I feel overwhelmed by the events and emotions of the day. I'm swept away before I hardly know what has happened. Can You give me some suggestions as to how to go about this?"

"Yes, I can give you a couple of simple tips. See if you can follow them."

"Certainly, I will try."

"First, when you get up, smile, just smile for a while. And then continue to smile some more, just for the sake of smiling itself, and see what happens. You may find that that smile fills your being with joy. With very little effort you may discover that the joy stays with you for a good part of the day. Try it! There is practically no investment and the highest dividends!"

"Really! That sounds very encouraging!"

"Here is another tip: Try to be aware and appreciative of

all the little things you take for granted. For instance, if you go for a walk, you may look at the flowers and allow yourself to marvel at their beautiful colors. At the same time, remind yourself of the pain they have necessarily gone through coming to blossom. Look at the pebbles, and see that they are as great as the great ascetics, completely unfazed by heat and cold, wind and rain. They will show you how to take life as it comes, unmoved and unaffected by either sorrow or delight. An awareness of such things gives you a receptivity to the silent messages which reveal the inner wonders of life. This will help you journey toward that continual happiness you are seeking."

"How wonderful it would be to wake with a smile, and take the kind of walk You describe!"

"This ever-so-brief life of the day should be a constant experiment in relation to the greater life," You added. "Unbinding moments, fresh and renewing, show you the true beauty of the greater life. However, you must not become attached to those moments which you consider to be the 'best.' These very moments may become like golden chains, which will fetter you, and hold you back in your journey to Me. Walk on, go on. But also remember that though you believe yourself to be seeking happiness, it is in fact the Ocean of happiness and bliss within you that is seeking you. This is the irony of life."

There was silence again. I thought about trying to formulate an amusing remark, but instead, too moved for that, I said to You, "It is Your presence that gives me the brightest smile."

It seemed I could feel Your breath beneath mine, as You were sitting so close to me. You looked deep into my eyes, and that silent response meant more to me than words could ever convey. I was pulled within, into a state of reverie. Then You patted my shoulder, and a surge of vitality flowed through me.

I wanted to express my gratitude to You in some way. Just then, a blossom fell from the branch hanging above us. Taking my eyes off You for just a moment, I bent down to pick it up as a humble offering to You. When I turned back, You had already gone. As I looked around, unknowingly I was led to the base of the tree trunk behind the bench. I lovingly knelt and placed the blossom there, in hopes that it would be accepted by You, the Root of all life. As I got up I felt that the flowers and pebbles on the path were reflecting Your lively smile.

The Full Moon's Grace

I was sitting all alone, late at night, on a small balcony attached to my room at an ocean resort. I sat on one of the two reclining chairs and looked over the long strand of beach, the line of waves breaking on the shore and the luminous light of the moon dancing on the water. I had come here for a long-overdue holiday and was having a most relaxing vacation.

It was so quiet and peaceful all around that there seemed nothing to disturb the captivating atmosphere. Yet, strangely enough, I began to feel restless. My mind raced feverishly through the events of my life related to various worldly activities. My thoughts kept whirling, and I felt a strange uneasiness come over me. A sense of hollowness welled up within me and gnawed at my heart. Perhaps everyone has a hole within them which is never filled or completely healed. And, from time to time, this inner void swallows the joy of living and robs one's peace of mind.

"What is this game that is being played through measure-less time and in unbounded space? Is there such a thing as time passing through space? Or is space an illusion devoured by time?" Such thoughts and many more made my head spin. In spite of knowing the limits of my abilities, periodically I have found myself wandering over the edge, in vain pursuit of answers to such questions. In the abstract, such speculations can sometimes be fun, but at other times they are very disturb-ing. And that night I was unable to curb my mind from trying to penetrate the mystery of time and space that had so tightly caged me.

Physically I was in good shape and I was not facing any serious problems, but paradoxically, this relative sense of well-being only seemed to accelerate and animate the functioning of my unbridled thoughts and feelings.

While my head was reeling, I turned to my right and saw You comfortably lounging on the other chair. With a natural grace and a glint of humor in Your eyes, You asked, "What has happened? Why do you look so dazed?"

Finding You there was a marvelous, breathtaking moment for me, and I simply stared at You in wonder and joy. Then, gesturing toward the vast expanse of the sky overhead and the ocean below, I said, "What's all this — this game going on in immeasurable time and unbounded space?"

With dignified composure, You replied, "It's a passing show of impermanence."

"And what will happen if and when time and space are totally absent?" I inquired.

"Deep, sound sleep in the immensity of the Nothing," You leisurely answered.

Although I did not at all understand, I persisted, "And if time and space and deep sleep too are in abeyance, what will exist?"

"The Infinity of the luminous consciousness of the Beyond," You promptly but gently replied.

All these states and statements were definitely beyond my comprehension. However, Your answers were so direct and poignant that to a great extent they calmed my tormented mind. I also felt that if someone else were to ask You these same questions, Your replies could be quite different. That would not surprise me, for Your approach is uniquely personal with each individual.

As I stared at You in amazement, I was enraptured by the serene beauty and lively tranquillity beaming from Your face. For some moments both of us remained silent, but somehow I was prompted to ask You the question that had been bothering me off and on regarding our earlier meetings. I sheepishly said, "How is it, after all the bliss and peace I have experienced during Your visits, I am still not totally certain about their validity? I still wonder whether these meetings with You are real or simply an imagined fantasy."

You gently touched me on the shoulder, and a thrill went

through my body. With a pleasant smile and peaceful intensity, You spoke: "These visits are as real and valid as your own thoughts and feelings. I am the Innermost You inviting you, through different doors, from different levels of your mind, to your Abode in Me." And you flashed a meaningful smile.

Moved by the impact of Your words, I answered, "Yes, whenever You visit me, I feel drenched in Your loving presence. But after You leave, my mind begins to think, 'How can a most finite individual like me ever really meet the Infinite One who is beyond time and space without losing my own individuality?' I can't explain what I feel within me after meeting You. For instance, how can a drop touch the Ocean and continue to retain its 'dropness'? This is an unsolvable dilemma."

I looked to You for some consolation, but You did not seem in the least affected by my problem, and with an easy smile You posed a counterquestion: "Why should these thoughts bother you? When the profundity of My presence has touched your heart through these visits, can't you simply brush away those doubting thoughts?"

I gulped in Your words and replied, "What You say is right, yet somehow it is not easy for me to wipe them out. My mind repeatedly insists on trying to ascertain whether these meetings are real or make-believe."

"They are both," You responded quite calmly.

"How can that be?" I asked, mystified.

In Your soft, unruffled way, You continued, "Reality is like the sun, which is self-evident. It needs no proof. However, in the light of the sun many things are made visible, and in this light the so-called opposites of beautiful and ugly, inviting and repellent can be seen — but in actuality they are not mutually exclusive. Reality is beyond intellectual comprehension, transcending countless states of experience. Long, wordy explanations only make things more complicated and confusing."

"So what is the way out?"

"Perhaps a simple analogy from daily life may give you a clue," You said.

"Tell me, I'm anxious to hear it!"

You looked at me with amusement and stood up. Touching the railing of the balcony and gesturing to the ocean beneath us, You said, "Can you see the way the moon is slowly descending to the horizon?"

"Yes, that is crystal-clear and also exquisitely beautiful."

Maintaining a serious look, You continued, "And you see the way the moon's resplendent light is reflected and refracted by the waves, casting a luminous sheen over the sea?"

"Yes," I answered. "It is marvelous."

"But it will last for only some hours longer. As the moon descends, the waves will seem to rise up toward it. When the moon reaches the horizon, it will appear as if the waves and the moon have fallen into each other's embrace. However, after some moments the moon will totally disappear and the water will look dark once more. Where has the light of the moon gone?"

I didn't know what to say, so I just set my eyes upon You. The sublimity of Your statement seemed to fill the silence around us. Then You smiled, Your face beaming like the full moon.

I was groping for a spark of understanding, but was failing. In fact, I could really neither follow nor fathom the depth of Your unique metaphor, but 'something,' unbeknownst to me, had filled the void within me with an indescribable peace. A luminous silence enveloped me as I gazed at You in wonder, but I could not utter a word.

Knowing full well my inner state of amazement and inability to speak, You gave me a tender look, and before I could catch my breath, You lovingly stated, "Calm down, don't be impatient. Love does not insist; it patiently waits. So try to resign to My will and try to be more and more aware of the uplifting feelings you experience whenever I visit you. Begin to absorb these in your life."

I nodded in deep reverence and gratitude, and although I did not comprehend at all the import of Your statements, nonetheless You wished to disclose a still deeper secret, for You continued: "You will not be able to anticipate the moment when your 'dropness' will burst and merge in the Ocean of My Reality. However, be sure that by My Grace it shall definitely happen at the opportune moment — the moment when the tide of your love and longing to find Union will rise and continue to rise so high that it touches the Full Moon of My Grace. This will be the moment when the drop of your false individuality, with the debris of its residual thoughts and feelings, will be ignited by the spark of My Grace and totally consumed in Me like a little granule of camphor.

"That will be both the beginning and the end of all words, of all conversations — in the shoreless Oceanity of My silence. It is the inconceivable Beyond state of My Being, wherein Existence and Nonexistence are eternally united. There is no full moon there, no rising tide of longing, neither drop nor ocean, but only the infinitude of My luminous Being that reigns from eternity to eternity."

Enraptured as I was by Your loving, enlightening words, I could hardly speak. As fresh tears of joy and gratitude cascaded down my cheeks, I felt You entered my heart, already so full, causing these words to overflow:

O Eternal Awakener,

You are in and beyond time and space.

But in Your infinite humor

You live in each moment

and are in everything;

no name or form can bind You,

yet any name or form can contain You totally.

O Real One, pull me into Your Being

to be united with You for all time

in Your immutable Silence.

This will be the miracle of

Your simple, unconditional Grace.

Amen!

Postscript

I am exceedingly touched by the many letters I have received from all over the world in response to my two previous books of *Conversations*. In these letters, readers shared the inner blossoming of their hearts, a springtide bestowed on them by The Awakener as they tried to relate more intimately to Him. I am moved to see how He opens the heart-portals of His dear ones, revealing His mysterious, loving presence ever residing within each one; this He does gracefully, in the most intimate, personal ways. I have seen how the reading of these conversations has inspired others to converse with Him in their daily living, in big and small matters alike.

I feel immensely indebted to The Awakener for His gifts of conversations to me. He is indeed the *Most Intimate One*. Through creative inner dialogues, He reveals, unfolds, and releases the true nature inherent in the very core of each one's being.

Some of the readers who have written to me have freely, in a very friendly manner, expressed how the reading of conversations has opened new inner dimensions in their relationship with the Compassionate One, who is anxious to guide and converse with them in their daily lives. It is these responses that, to a great extent, have prompted me to venture into the writing of the present book, sharing my dialogues with The Awakener.

During a visit, a dear friend of mine, Kendra, once quietly handed me an envelope. Upon opening it, I was surprised by the contents: it was a conversation — what a wonderful treat! With her consent, I wish to share it, to give readers a brief glimpse of the heartwarming and heartfelt responses shared with me by my many friends after reading *Conversations*.

With deepest gratitude I offer my salutations to the
all-forgiving Father and all-loving Mother —
The Awakener. May He bless us and guide us with
His ever-renewing presence toward our final and
inseparable Union with Him.

A Little Chat

"Oh Lord, Bal's conversations are so wonderful. I wish that I too could learn the art of conversing with You."

"Why shouldn't you? Everyone and anyone can converse with Me."

"Well, I've tried talking to You, but I don't seem to get any reply. That puts a damper on the conversation rather quickly."

"Have you considered that the art of conversation is really the art of listening?"

"Maybe I haven't learned that lesson yet. I do try to listen, but usually all I hear is my own thoughts. The parade of cynical, vain, and doubting comments is a long one, and though I try to let each horn-blowing irrelevancy go by, immediately another one comes along, beating a drum."

"For ages you have been a spectator at the passing show of the mind. Now it is time to turn away from the spectacle and attend only to My eternal presence."

"If I do that, will I begin to hear You speaking to me?"

"Better than that, you will begin to feel and hear My silence. Hearing it, you will draw deeper into its depths, until you live and breathe My silent Ocean of Love."

"And drown in it?"

"When the time is right. But for now, why not just enjoy our little chat? I will tell you one more secret about the art of conversation with Me. Don't think that My replies come only in words.

"Your very life, with all its ordinary tasks and everyday activities, is My conversation with you. If you attend closely, you will receive My companionship and guidance through each experience and event. For I am the One who is ever speaking through My creation — and ever silent in the heart of My perfect Lover."

—K.C.B.

On Conversations

Excerpts from the author's replies
in response to letters received on *Conversations*

The Source of these conversations with the ever-renewing Awakener, the One residing in each one's being, is unconditional Love which sustains life. This Love is all the time waiting for the slightest genuine response from the heart, and the conversation begins.

❧

I am like a crooked dried twig on The Awakener's universal tree. When the bird — the presence of The Awakener — comes and perches on the twig, it gradually comes to life, and buds sprout. The tender shoots and leaves with their lovely soft colors appear. They begin to rustle in harmony with all the other leaves on the tree and with the tree as a whole. These song-like rustlings and movements form a conversation.

When the bird flies away, the twig returns to its former

shape and state. Every conversation has deepened my trust that I am His dry twig — that I belong to The Awakener.

As for when the conversations began, it is hard for me to pinpoint a specific moment or episode. If you ask me specific details about a particular conversation, I will be able to describe only the general idea of it. It is as though I had been walking in the Garden of The Awakener, taking in the fragrance and beauty of the place, which had filled my heart. And every time I entered the garden, I went by a different gate, and each time He was there to greet me, to enlighten and pacify me. Though I no longer recollect by which gate I first entered this blessed garden, these visits have transformed my life.

A conversation is my play with The Awakener's presence, and at the same time, a game that He plays with me. In the beginning, I clearly view a sunlit peak, but do not know how to scale it, how to reach the top. Or sometimes I hear a piece of a refrain, or a rhythm, but do not find the words or notes to make a melodious song out of it. However, through the suspense and uncertainty of this playful challenge, my feeling of intimacy with Him blossoms. It exerts a tender pull, leading me to the melodies that contribute to forming a conversation. However, I often wonder whether I have succeeded in presenting it in the way He expects of me!

The writing of *Conversations* is not the result of inspiration or intuition. It is a wee bit of recognition (not revelation) of my relationship with the Eternal Awakener, my Father and Mother in One. I am happy to admit that the conversations form a most delightful part of my life with Him, a way to be in His close presence. The conversations are neither totally "real" nor completely "fictional." The percentage of "truth" contained in them is for the readers to decide and judge. And I assure you that I will not disagree or argue with anyone about their judgment.

Will you please treat me as one of your friends who is willing to correct himself? For I do not claim to understand all that is stated in these conversations. This book is just an elementary attempt to share something that has moved my heart, and which I was unable to keep to myself.

With best wishes and much love in The Awakener eternally residing in you.

All Glory to Him!